Teen Survival Guides

Learning to Self-Manage

JENNIFER SANDERSON

CHERITON
CHILDREN'S BOOKS

Published in 2026 by **Cheriton Children's Books**
1 Bank Drive West, Shrewsbury, Shropshire, SY3 9DJ, UK

First Edition

Author: Jennifer Sanderson
Designer: Paul Myerscough
Editor: Kelly Short
Proofreader: Amy Strauss

Picture credits: Cover: Shutterstock/Billion Photos. Inside: p4: Shutterstock/BigPixel Photo, p5: Shutterstock/Fizkes, p6: Shutterstock/Mangostar, p8: Shutterstock/Monkey Business Images, p9: Shutterstock/Antonio Guillem, p11: Shutterstock/Shisu Ka, p13: Shutterstock/DimaBerlin, p14: Shutterstock/Ground Picture, p15: Shutterstock/Antonio Guillem, p16: Shutterstock/Cookie Studio, p17: Shutterstock/Branislav Nenin, p19: Shutterstock/Chay Tee, p20: Shutterstock/Golden Pixels LLC, p21: Shutterstock/Fizkes, p23: Shutterstock/Halfpoint, p24: Shutterstock/Fizkes, p25: Shutterstock/Connect Images/Curated, p27: Shutterstock/Branislav Nenin, p28: Shutterstock/AYO Production, p29: Shutterstock/Sirtravelalot, p30: Shutterstock/Geraino812, p31: Shutterstock/PeopleImages.com/Yuri A, p33: Shutterstock/Andrey Yurlov, p34: Shutterstock/Fizkes, p35: Shutterstock/Fizkes, p36: Shutterstock/GaudiLab, p37: Shutterstock/Prostock Studio, p38: Shutterstock/Nakhshkarian Narine, p39: Shutterstock/Trzykropy, p40: Shutterstock/Monkey Business Images, p41: Shutterstock/Antonio Guillem, p42: Shutterstock/Jacob Lund, p43: Shutterstock/Tint Media, p45: Shutterstock/Josep Suria, p46: Shutterstock/Raul Mellado Ortiz, p47: Shutterstock/G-Stock Studio, p48: Shutterstock/Davide Angelini, p49: Shutterstock/Nomad Soul, p51: Shutterstock/Polya Olya, p52: Shutterstock/Monkey Business Images, p53: Shutterstock/Ground Picture, p54: Shutterstock/Rawpixel.com, p55: Shutterstock/T.Vyc, p57: Shutterstock/Dragana Gordic, p58: Shutterstock/VH Studio, p59: Shutterstock/Dmytro Zinkevych.

Printed in China

Please visit our website,
www.cheritonchildrensbooks.com
to see more of our high-quality books.

Contents

INTRODUCTION

Managing Yourself

Think back to when you were ten years old. Then, your life was probably quite straightforward. That may be because most of the time your parents/caregivers, teachers, and other adults told you what to do and helped you make many of your decisions. You probably had a routine that included a homework time and a bedtime, and there may have been strict rules about what you could and couldn't do. Although that wasn't long ago, things likely changed when you became a teenager. Now, your life has probably become quite different.

Part of Growing Up

When you enter the teen years, your body changes. For a start, gone are your baby features! And as your body changes on the outside, internal change is taking place too. All this change is because your hormones are making you look different, and think and feel differently too. Physically and emotionally you're on your way to becoming an adult. Because you look different, you may feel much more grown up and want to do things independently of your parents and siblings. However, until you're much older, you may not be ready to be as independent as you'd like to be. More importantly, independence doesn't just happen overnight—there are skills you need to understand and master first. And these skills can be placed under the umbrella of self-management.

When you become a teen, your parents have to start letting go. They have to trust you to be more independent as you spend more time outside the home, perhaps in a job.

STUDIES IN TEEN SURVIVAL

Adolescence is a time of huge change—physically, mentally, and emotionally. At this time, people are trying to figure out their identities, what they believe in, and what their values are. They might be more impulsive too. All this can make self-management difficult.

It's tough being a teenager and things can often get pretty heated. Learning to stay calm in a difficult situation is a self-management skill that is worth mastering.

Skills for Life

Self-management is key to independence. However, it's about more than simply getting on with things on your own. It's about making informed decisions, handling responsibility, and taking charge of your life. In this book, we'll look at ten self-management skills that are important to master now, while you're a teenager. If you can get a handle on them now, it will make being an adult much easier. These skills are:

- **Accountability**
- **Regulating emotions**
- **Adaptability**
- **Goal setting**
- **Self-motivation**
- **Time management**
- **Stress management**
- **Self-care**
- **Decision making**
- **Community belonging**

We'll explain what these terms mean as we work through the book and explore them in workshops. By the time you've finished the book, you'll understand what they mean. Even better, you'll have learned some important self-management skills—skills you can use for the rest of your life.

CHAPTER 1

Owning It

Admitting you're wrong and saying sorry is the first step toward resolving a conflict.

You may have grand plans in your head, you may even have written these down (we'll talk more about this later in the book). Sometimes, though, things don't work out the way we want them to or how we planned. Perhaps, you have done something that didn't work out because you made a mistake. Realizing and then owning up to these setbacks—as well as your successes—is called being accountable. By being accountable, you're taking responsibility for your actions and thoughts. You're doing what you set out to do, fulfilling your obligations, and achieving your goals, without excuses or blaming others.

Teen Need to Know

No one is perfect, and by being accountable you're not striving for perfection. Let's take a live sports match as an example. If you've ever watched one live, did each player do things perfectly? If they did, there wouldn't be much of a contest! Sportspeople are human, just like everyone else: They drop balls, they fall over, and sometimes, there are better players on opposing teams. Mistakes are all part of life, but how you manage them makes the difference between winning and losing.

Let's look at the sports team idea again to see how this works. When teams practice, they do so with mistakes in mind. They have a plan B in case things go wrong. And when things go wrong, they use plan B to give it their all and to put their mistake behind them. And the very same technique can be used when it comes to managing daily life. It always helps to have a plan B.

It's Important...

You may ask why being accountable is important. Isn't it just easier to blame someone else and move on? It may seem attractive to hand over the blame to other people when things go wrong, but while that may seem to benefit you, it actually doesn't. You might be wondering how that works! Well, by being accountable, you'll realize that every action has a consequence, whether it's a good or bad outcome. If it's a good one, that's great. You'll know what you're doing next time around so you get the same positive result. But what if the consequence turns out to be not so good?

...But It's Difficult

If your action has a negative consequence, you'll need to deal with that, and that can be really difficult. It's hard to admit you did something wrong, especially when other people are involved. However, this is part of the learning experience. By dealing with the negative consequences of your actions, you will be able to find a better solution to the problem next time around. You will hopefully learn from your mistake so that you don't repeat it. Sometimes, it may take a few attempts to get things right, but as long as you do, that's what matters. By owning up when things go wrong and you make a mistake, your relationships will be healthier too. People will appreciate your honesty and are more likely to forgive and forget than if you blame them for your own mistakes.

A PROBLEM-BUSTING TOOL

Being Honest with Yourself

It can be hard to own up to mistakes and take accountability for them if you are not only dishonest with others, but also not honest with yourself. It's easy to tell yourself that you've done nothing wrong, but you'll likely feel bad later. By being honest with yourself and others, you'll feel better about yourself long term.

Let's Talk about Accountability

Part of being accountable is acknowledging your strengths and weaknesses. Your strengths are things you do well and your weaknesses are the things you need to work on a little (or sometimes, a lot!). Understanding your weaknesses is vital if you're going to be accountable. That's because when you understand your weaknesses, you can ask for help. Asking for help is not showing weakness—in fact, it takes strength of character to be accountable and admit that you need help.

When you know your strengths and weaknesses, you can get the help you need, whether it's to improve your grades or do better at a sport.

Defining Self-Management Skills: Accountability

Being accountable is not just about owning your thoughts or actions. It's about learning from mistakes so that you can do better in the future. When things don't go according to plan, and you're given feedback, dealing with this is also part of being accountable.

THE SELF-MANAGEMENT WORKSHOP

Not Being Accountable

If you don't take accountability, it can create problems. For example, imagine that you have a mid-semester math test coming up. You know you need to do well in it. So, you get your books together and start revising. But then your phone pings. There's a message from your friend. You reply, then your friend messages back, and soon what was a quick question turns into a big chat. You finally finish chatting, but you find it really hard to get back into your revision.

The test is difficult, much harder than you thought it would be. When you check your paper, you haven't done well at all. That upsets you, and you tell your mom, "It was really hard and besides, my teacher never even spent time in class revising." Your mom makes you promise to ask your teacher for help. She also says you need to study harder for the next test. But you don't do either. And you don't do well in the next test too.

THE SELF-MANAGEMENT WORKSHOP

Same situation, but with accountability.

Taking Ownership

When your phone pings, you spend time chatting with your friend, but you find it really hard to get back into your revision. The test is difficult. When you check your paper, you haven't done well at all. That upsets you, and you tell your mom, "I really didn't work hard enough. But don't worry, I have a plan." You ask your teacher for help, you work on your math each day, and because your phone is switched off, you aren't distracted. By the time the next test comes around, you do a lot better.

What Works Better Here?:

- You take ownership for your studying.
- You realize you are being distracted and instead of blaming others, you think about things and get a plan of action together.
- You ask your teacher for help with your work.
- You study more each day, without distractions.

Being Accountable—What Can It Do for You?

Have you ever been in a situation like this? Did you take ownership of your mistakes? What have you learned and what would you do differently if a similar situation comes up in the future? Instead of making excuses, when you're accountable, you figure out what is a genuine weakness. You check where you went wrong so that you can learn from your mistakes. Accountability also means not blaming others. This will improve your relationships because you won't blame others for things that are not their fault.

Being accountable will help you better manage your studies, and other areas of your life too.

A PROBLEM-BUSTING TOOL

Learning from Mistakes

Everyone makes mistakes, and mistakes are part of life. When you work on being more accountable, you'll start to figure out where you went wrong. One way to do this is to really think about the consequences of actions by asking yourself these three questions:

- What went wrong?
- Why did it go wrong?
- How can I do better next time?

When you know the answer to these questions, you can figure out a plan to do better in the future.

WHY SELF-MANAGEMENT WORKS

Just as you'd use the correct tools to fix something that's broken, self-management is all about using the right tools for the job. Let's take another look at why being accountable is so important.

1 Being Accountable Builds Good Decision Making

When you are accountable, you take ownership of the consequences of your actions. Knowing the consequences of an action will help you make the right decision when you have to.

2 Accountable People Learn from Their Mistakes

It's OK to make mistakes—everyone does. But you need to own up to your mistakes and learn from them if you make them.

3 Accountability Builds Stronger Relationships

If you don't blame others for your faults, you will build healthier relationships.

4 Discover Your Strengths and Weaknesses

If you are honest with yourself, you will soon know your strengths and weaknesses. This means you'll know to ask for help when you need it.

It's OK to Be Wrong

You've heard this before: It's OK to not be perfect. There will be times when you get things wrong (even very wrong). But if you look inward, you'll see how you can do things differently the next time, and you'll soon know when to ask for help if you need it.

CHAPTER 2

You and Your Family: A Survival Guide

Today's families come in different shapes and sizes. For example, in your household, you may live with both parents and a sibling or two. But your friend's parents may be divorced or separated, and your friend may live with a stepfather when they are at their mother's house or a stepmother and stepsibling when at their father's home. Living under one roof with a mix of people, each with their own personality, can be difficult. But it's even more so when you're a teenager. And in this chapter we'll explain why.

What Your Parents Think

You're growing up and feel like you are ready to take on the world, but your parents may still see you as a child. That's because whether you're a new-born, toddler, teenager, or adult, you are still your parents' child. They have watched you grow from being a tiny baby to a curious toddler, and now, you want to be an independent young adult. This can be hard because every parent wants to protect their child. They'll find it difficult to watch you make mistakes, especially those that are preventable, because they want the best for you.

When different generations of the same family come together, it can be a great way for everyone to get along.

What You Think

While your parents may hate the thought of you growing up and not needing them, you most likely can't wait to be independent. You are probably clashing and arguing a lot more with your parents and siblings. This may be because you feel more grown up, and you are forming your own opinions and ideas about things. These ideas may be very different from those of your parents. Then add a sibling into the mix. Perhaps you clash when you borrow their clothes or they get annoyed because you no longer want to hang out with them. With all these family tensions, things can get pretty heated.

Not all siblings see eye to eye all the time. As you and your siblings grow up, clashes are inevitable.

Independence NOW!

Your homelife doesn't need to be difficult, though. If your parents can see that you're developing the skills needed to be more independent and that you're learning as you develop, they are more likely to cut you some slack. The self-management skills that most affect family life are being able to regulate your emotions and being adaptable.

STUDIES IN TEEN SURVIVAL

Families are changing all the time and many children come from blended families. According to a recent US Census Bureau, more than 2.3 million parents stated that their child lived with a stepbrother or stepsister. Living in a blended family can be difficult, especially if you don't get on with your stepsiblings or stepparent. If that is the case, you can make it easier on yourself and other family members if you work on your self-management skills, especially those that have an effect on your whole family.

Being a teenager can be like being on a roller coaster. There are ups and downs and twists and turns. That can make your life fun but also scary at the same time.

An Emotional Roller Coaster

An emotion is something you feel. Some emotions, like happiness, gratitude, and excitement, leave you feeling good inside and great about yourself. But others, such as anger and frustration, can make you want to lash out. Afterward, you probably don't feel very good about yourself. As a teenager, you're likely feeling a lot more emotional than you did as a younger child. That means you can experience a lot of lows and highs—and everything in between—and all of them in a single day.

Let's Talk about Regulating Emotions

While some emotions, like happiness and joy, feel better than others, there are no right or wrong emotions. You cannot help how you feel. However, how you deal with your emotions affects both you and those around you. That includes your parents and siblings. So, to help better manage your life at home, you need to learn to regulate your emotions.

Defining Self-Management Skills: Regulating Emotions

Being able to regulate your emotions is one of the most important self-management skills. Regulating your emotions means managing how you feel in response to situations. This means keeping your emotions in check so that you stay calm. And when you're calm, you will be able to communicate more effectively. That helps you build healthier, stronger relationships.

THE SELF-MANAGEMENT WORKSHOP

Out-of-Control Emotions

There are always going to be tricky situations to manage in your life, along with feelings that can seem overwhelming. That's just all part of daily life. However, with self-regulation, everything is manageable. But what happens when you let your emotions run wild?

Imagine this scenario: Your friend is turning 16 and having a big party. All your friends are going. You know you need to ask your parents' permission to go. Usually, they say yes, so you are pretty sure they'll agree. You say, "Dad, is it OK if I go to the party next weekend? All my friends are going." Your dad knows it means a lot to you, so he agrees. But he adds, "I'll fetch you at 10:30." You feel annoyed. You don't see why you need a curfew. You don't want to miss out on any of the party. You get angry and shout, "That's so unfair! All my friends are staying until 12."

Sometimes, you may feel that your parents are treating you like a baby, but shouting and screaming isn't going to make them treat you like a responsible teenager. By learning to regulate your emotions, you'll be able to handle situations like this a lot better...

THE SELF-MANAGEMENT WORKSHOP

Same situation, but with better control.

Getting a Handle on Emotions

Your friend is turning 16 and having a big party. You know you need to ask your parents' permission to go. You say, "Dad, is it OK if I go to the party next weekend? All my friends are going." Your dad agrees. But he adds, "I'll fetch you at 10:30." You feel annoyed, but you ask, "Why do I need such an early curfew? All my friends are staying until after 12." Your dad explains that the curfew is there because he and your mom need to know when to expect you home and so they won't be kept up late, worrying until you get back. You think about it and ask, "Can we maybe do 11 instead?" Your dad smiles and says, "Sure, OK."

What Works Better Here?:

- You manage to keep your emotions in check and show your dad respect by asking politely why you need such an early curfew. You allow him to give his answer.
- You explain the reasons why you want to stay out later.
- When your dad explains his point of view, you listen carefully and calmly. You can see his viewpoint.
- Because you keep calm, your dad feels as though you are listening to his point of view. He is then willing to compromise on the time, and you find a solution.

Emotional Regulation—What Can It Do for You?

Yelling and shouting at your parents shows you aren't listening to their side of an argument. When you stay calm and express your feelings and thoughts clearly and with consideration and respect for others, you are more likely to be listened to and a compromise can be reached.

Listening to the other side of an argument helps keep the channels of communication open.

A PROBLEM-BUSTING TOOL

Keeping Calm in a Storm

When emotions are high, it's easy to overreact and feel angry and frustrated with others. Recognizing what triggers feelings of anger is important. Although you can't always avoid frustrating situations, you can learn how to react to them in a way that isn't angry. When you first start to feel angry, instead of lashing out, take a deep breath and count to ten in your head. Often, this small pause will help you calm down and cause a break in your reaction. That then allows you to diffuse the situation and make your case without an emotional outburst.

Step this way for more great ways you can keep calm in a difficult situation.

Other Ways to Calm Things Down

Counting to ten is just one way to stop yourself from flying into a rage. There are other ways to keep calm and diffuse a tricky situation. They include the helpful, calm-inducing strategies below:

- **Making a choice about how to respond:** Rather than losing control of your emotions, try telling someone how you feel. Try to use an "I feel" statement, for example, "I feel angry because..."
- **Look for the positive emotion:** People are often far quicker to acknowledge their negative emotions than their positive ones. Try to make a habit of noticing when you feel content, grateful, or at peace. Then think about what you can do to feel like this more often.
- **Talk to yourself:** When you feel upset or frustrated, instead of blaming yourself or others, use what you've learned about being accountable. Try telling yourself, "I've tried hard, maybe next time I'll..." Instead of blaming someone else who has made a mistake, rather think, "People are doing the best they can."

Your siblings may annoy you, but keeping calm in a conflict is good for your relationship.

The Value of a Calm Head

Anger-management strategies sound great in theory. However, it can be really difficult to keep calm, especially when those around you are not. But there are several benefits to keeping a cool head in a conflict. Keeping calm helps you think logically and make a thought-through decision. It keeps you aware and focused so you can think clearly. Keeping calm is also good for communication—rather than having an argument, you can have a discussion. Because people tend to talk faster when they're yelling, being calm gives you time to prepare before you speak. And that helps you say the right thing.

Teen Need to Know

Did you know, the teen brain is not yet fully developed? The front part of the brain still has some growing to do, so teenagers rely on the more primitive back part of the brain to interpret people's facial expressions. This part of the brain is the first to pick up on danger and threat. It is trained to detect hostile emotions. Sometimes, the brain picks up on these emotions, even when they aren't actually present. That is why it's important to take a deep breath before you launch into an argument.

The human brain isn't fully developed until someone is in their mid-to-late 20s. So until then, people's facial expressions may be a bit difficult to figure out.

A PROBLEM-BUSTING TOOL

Journaling

One of the best ways to really understand your emotions is to write about them in a journal. Journaling helps you understand what has triggered each emotion. If you understand why you feel a certain way, you'll react more calmly and in a more-regulated way.

Let's Talk about Adaptability

One of the words that seems to come up a lot when people talk about teenagers is "change." People may tell you that there are hormones running through your body, causing physical changes and emotional changes. You may start to think and feel differently —perhaps things you've always liked are no longer your favorites.

Your family may be changing too. A grandparent may have passed away or perhaps you have a new sibling or a stepsibling. Change can be really tough, and that's where the next self-management skill comes in—adaptability. Learning to be adaptable will help you deal with all the changes that come your way. By being adaptable, you'll be able to adjust course and find a new pathway forward, no matter what curve balls life happens to throw your way.

Defining Self-Management Skills: Adaptability

Adaptability means being able to adjust to changes in your environment and respond to new information. Being adaptable also means thinking about how changes will affect you and those around you. Sometimes, a change may feel more difficult for you than it does for a sibling or parent. Learning to be adaptable means thinking about how you can embrace the change rather than feel your life has been turned inside-out because of it.

STUDIES IN TEEN SURVIVAL

Sometimes, people are forced to adapt quickly to a new situation. For example, if someone becomes sick, they may have to take time off school or college. They may have to do a lot of their learning at home. They may have to use technology to complete their lessons, work, and communicate with their friends and family.

Being forced to adapt is not always easy. However, studies show that students who are more adaptable than others show greater depth of learning in challenging situations. They are also more motivated. This means that they want to achieve the goals they set.

Occasionally, homeschooling is necessary. But it can create tension in the house as everyone adapts to the situation.

Accept What You Cannot Change

Once you've thought through the changes, you may realize that there's nothing you can do but accept them. Some things are beyond your control. For example, if your parent gets a new job and you have to relocate to a new state, there's not a lot you can do about it. Sure, you can yell about how unfair life is and how you are not going. However, the reality is that this type of behavior won't change anything—it'll probably just make your parents upset and angry. Instead, you can try to better understand their reasons for taking the new job and the relocation. The new job may mean a promotion, which in turn means a better salary and more perks. The relocation may also mean being closer to other family members or a better school for you.

The Benefits of Being Adaptable

In addition to being more motivated, being adaptable has other benefits too. Being adaptable and able to adjust means you will be able to learn new skills more easily. Sometimes, to embrace change, you have to learn how to do something that's new to you. It may take a while to get the hang of the new skill, but if you persevere, you'll get there. When you realize that you've accepted the change and have adapted to the new situation, you'll likely look back and feel proud of yourself. If you are happy with how you've dealt with something, it will give your self-confidence a big boost too.

When you make a mistake, don't give up. Try instead to persevere and keep going. You'll be glad that you did.

Building Resilience

Being adaptable goes hand in hand with being resilient. But what is resilience? It is being able to bounce back after a challenge. It's being able to pick up the pieces and carry on, even when times are tough. It's not always easy to do this, and being resilient won't make your problems go away. However, it will enable you to see past the problems. Once you see and understand how the problems fit into the bigger picture, you can better work through them.

At first, you may not like that something has changed. But, in time, you'll get used to it and will probably be happier for it.

A Problem-Busting Tool

Dealing with Change

Sometimes, things go your way and you can easily adapt to the change. But what if the change is more of a curve ball and turns your life upside down? You can still deal with it, and here are five ways to embrace the change and be more adaptable:

- **Embrace uncertainty:** Unless you can predict the future, you won't know exactly what's coming your way. Instead of letting your mind run wild with worry, try to understand that you cannot control everything. You may just have to go with the flow instead and see how things pan out.
- **Seek out change:** Change what you can to get the result you want. Don't sit back and wait for change to happen—make it happen!
- **Develop a growth mindset:** A growth mindset means to want to grow and change as a person. If you put in the effort and persevere with any given task, you will succeed. It may not happen immediately, but you will get there.
- **Be willing to do things differently:** You don't always have to do things in exactly the same way. Sometimes, by doing things a little differently, you'll see things in a new light and gain a new perspective.

WHY SELF-MANAGEMENT WORKS

Learning to self-manage is complicated and affects everyone in a family. This chapter has looked at two tools to help develop self-management skills: regulating emotions and adaptability.

1 Understanding Emotions Helps You Keep Calm

There are no right or wrong emotions. Learning to regulate your emotions means keeping calm in a storm.

2 Keeping Calm Leads to Good Communication

By keeping calm, it's possible to have discussions rather than arguments with family members. Being calm also helps you communicate more effectively. When you are able to say how you feel, you are more likely to be listened to.

3 Being Adaptable Helps You Manage Change

Change can be difficult, especially when a lot of change is taking place at the same time. However, by being resilient and learning to cope with change when it happens, it doesn't feel as daunting.

4

You Can Learn from Failure

Everyone fails and no one ever gets everything right the first time. Learning from mistakes and not being too hard on yourself builds resilience and determination.

Lifelong Learning

Learning to regulate your emotions and to be more adaptable when things don't go as planned are key skills to help you deal with any family situation. These skills are not just for now—you'll be able to use them throughout your life in many different situations.

CHAPTER 3

School, College, and Work

Being a teenager is the start of spending less time with your family and more time in the outside world. That means more time away from the comfort and security of your home and the things that are so familiar to you. Suddenly, you'll find that you're spending more and more time at school, where the hours may be long and tiring.

The Life of a Teenager

School can be tough! You have coursework to complete, important tests to study for, and maybe sports or club activities to practice for. Sometimes, it may seem every teacher or coach thinks their subject or activity is the most important of all. That may leave you feeling overwhelmed. And that's before you even start to deal with a weekend job and fit in your busy social life. But there is an upside to all these new demands. You can use managing your time at school and college to help you prepare for the pressures you'll later face at work.

Life can be challenging at times, but once you master some basic self-management skills, you'll be on the path to success.

Life as a teenager can feel chaotic. But if you're organized, you'll bring calm to any situation.

Developing New Skills

Managing demands to achieve a more balanced work life requires some key skills. These include goal setting, self-motivation, time management, stress management, and self-care. If you can master these skills, you will be well prepared to face the day-to-day demands of school and college before you head off into the workplace.

Build Some Lists

Most of the tools you're going to learn in this chapter are about being organized and making lists and schedules. This list building may seem like work at first. However, by building lists, you are structuring your thoughts. You're also giving yourself the chance to rethink them. You may find it helpful to have a special book in which you can write down the lists you're going to make. There are also some useful list-building apps that can help you stay on top of things.

Teen Need to Know

Researchers say that adults spend around one-third of their waking hours at work. That's a lot of time spent away from home. Imagine if you are unhappy at work—you'd be spending a lot of time being miserable. One way to remedy this is to work on self-management skills to help you lead a fulfilled work life. But, like all new skills, these tools don't just magically happen overnight. They take practice to master.

Let's Talk about Goal Setting

Goal setting is important because it keeps us focused on what is important to us. Think about your daily life and what you want to achieve. Do you have personal or academic goals, or both? Which of these goals is the most important?

Be SMART

Goals can be short term and achievable in the not-so-distant future. They can also be long term, and you'll work toward them over a longer time frame. Either way, one way to set goals is to use the SMART framework. SMART goals are specific, measurable, achievable, relevant, and time-bound. Here's how they work:

- **Specific goals:** Think about what you need to do. What do you have to do to achieve this?
- **Measurable goals:** By having a measurable goal, you can track your progress.
- **Achievable goals:** Be realistic. Is your goal achievable?
- **Relevant goals:** Understand why you are setting the goal.
- **Time-bound goals:** Know how long you have to achieve the goal.

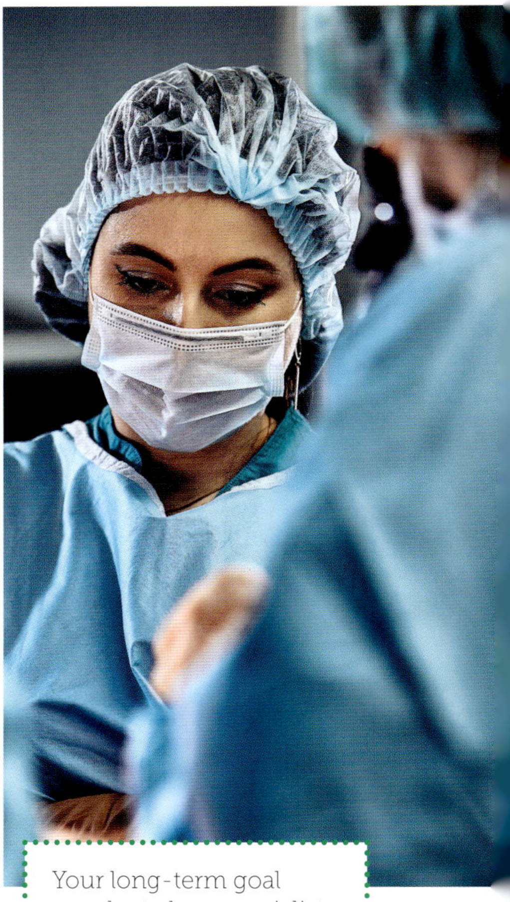

Your long-term goal may be to be a specialist surgeon. However, to achieve it, you'll need to set short-term goals to get you into med school.

Defining Self-Management Skills: Goal Setting

By figuring out what you'd like to achieve, personally and in your school life, you'll likely realize that your goals are unique to you. You are not competing with anyone else, only yourself. If you set SMART goals for each aspect of your life, you'll be a well-rounded individual. You won't be perfect, but you'll be the best version of yourself. Each step you take toward achieving your goal will create a big impact.

THE SELF-MANAGEMENT WORKSHOP

Goals That Aren't SMART

It can be far more difficult to get to where you want to be without SMART goals. For example, imagine that you want to be on the swim team. So you start your training program. But you haven't really thought through your schedule. You just go to the pool every day and swim a few different strokes.

The day of the team trials quickly comes around. You stand on the blocks, ready for the first race. It's breaststroke—your worst stroke. As the buzzer goes off, you dive in and do your best. But when you reach the other end of the pool, you realize you haven't done enough to make the team. You feel upset, and decide not to do any further trials. You don't want to fail again.

What went wrong here? You set a very broad goal and did not think carefully about what exactly you hoped to achieve. Perhaps if you had picked just your best stroke to work on, you could have made the swim team. Let's take a look overleaf at the value of setting SMART goals.

THE SELF-MANAGEMENT WORKSHOP

Same situation, but SMARTER!

Setting SMART Goals

You decide you want to be on the swim team. You think about what your two best strokes are and ask a friend to time your laps. You set the goal of taking four seconds off your freestyle time and two off your butterfly time. You set a training schedule. You work on your stroke to make yourself a better swimmer.

The day of the team trials comes around quickly. You stand on the blocks, ready for your first race. It is freestyle. As the gun goes off, you dive in. When you reach the other end of the pool, you realize that you have set a PB and have come third! Next is the butterfly race. Although you don't do as well in the butterfly, you are proud of yourself. You plan to do even better next time.

What Works Better Here?:

- You look at your strengths and weaknesses.
- You pick your two best strokes to work on and set realistic goals that are achievable.
- You commit to a specific target time and then work hard to achieve this.
- You also ask for help from others.

Goal Setting—What Can It Do for You?

By setting a goal, you become focused and determined. You understand what is required and work on it. Goal setting teaches determination and perseverance. You have to work hard to achieve your goals, and sometimes, it takes time to reach your target. The key is to plan well and keep going.

If you work consistently toward a goal, your hard work and dedication will pay off.

A PROBLEM-BUSTING TOOL

Dealing with Failure

Sometimes, things don't always go as planned and you don't achieve what you set out to. That can leave you feeling like a failure. When you feel like this, think about what went wrong. Be accountable and understand what you can do differently next time around. Don't give up either. Instead, maybe revaluate your goals and go back to the A in SMART. Set a more achievable, realistic goal and try again, turning your failure into a goal-setting opportunity. Understand that YET is key: You may not have reached your target YET, but you will if you persevere.

Let's Talk about Self-Motivation

Setting goals is important, but so too is persevering to reach them. It's not always easy to feel like doing what you set out to do. Psychologists call this engagement versus escape. Instead of facing your challenges, sometimes, it's easier to escape—by avoiding them. For example, you could study or you could avoid your studies and watch all the latest reels on your phone.

It may be easier to put in the effort when there's a prize at stake. But what if there are no prizes and you still need to put in the effort?

Being Motivated

Sometimes, there are external factors that keep you motivated. There may be prize money at stake, or a medal or certificate. Your parents may realize that you are avoiding working on your goals. They may set rewards to motivate you, to keep you working and focused. But how do you stay engaged and focused when you aren't being rewarded by your teachers, coaches, or parents? The answer is self-motivation.

Defining Self-Management Skills: Self-Motivation

Self-motivation is having the drive within yourself to act, rather than always relying on others to motivate you. When you are self-motivated, you do things because you really want to. To motivate yourself, you need to know what your personal values and interests are. And when you know what matters most to you, you can set short-term and long-term goals to work on.

How to Motivate Yourself

One of the tricks to staying motivated is to keep your eye on the prize. Visualize your success and use positive mental imagery. If you can believe something, you can achieve it. Instead of going for one big goal, use your goal-setting skills to set smaller, achievable goals. The feeling of success when you reach a small goal will help keep you self-motivated.

To stay self-motivated, you also need to understand that there are consequences for your actions. For example, if you don't train, you won't stay in shape. Holding yourself accountable is key. It may be worth going back to chapter one of this book and reminding yourself how to develop your accountability skills.

STUDIES IN TEEN SURVIVAL

In a recent study, US teens aged 13 to 17 were asked to choose a statement that describes them well: "I need someone to motivate me," or "My motivation mostly comes from within." The majority—67 percent—said they are mostly self-motivated, while 32 percent said they need someone else to motivate them. When you set yourself a challenge, no matter how big or small, and you achieve your aim through hard work and self-motivation, it will give you a great feeling of achievement.

Being self-motivated will push you to work harder to achieve your goals.

Let's Talk about Time Management

Teenagers are usually really busy. Sometimes, it may feel like everyone is demanding something different of you and in particular, of your time. Your teachers expect certain grades, so you need to study. Your parents want you to spend time with them and time with your siblings. And your friends would like to see you more often. All these demands on your time can feel very overwhelming and that can lead to anxiety. There are only so many hours in the day, so how do you make sure you meet your deadlines and still find time to relax, eat, and sleep? Well, that's where time management comes in to play.

Defining Self-Management Skills: Time Management

Time management is planning and controlling how you spend your time to accomplish goals. You've learned how to set goals, but now you need to be able to prioritize which goals are more important and which ones need more time spent on them. This will mean that you have to plan ahead and be organized about how much time you allocate to all the things you need to do, or want to do, every day.

There are only 24 hours in each day. How can you possibly fit in everything?! It can feel alarming to think about the many different tasks or activities you need to fit in to your day, but it becomes less scary and more achievable with time management.

Being Organized Feels Great!

Not everyone is naturally organized. Some people lead a disorganized lifestyle, and that's fine if it works for them. However, being disorganized comes with its own set of problems, including unnecessary stress and anxiety. It's much better for your emotional and physical wellbeing to be organized and to be able to manage your time effectively. This will help you keep focused, and when you're focused, there's less chaos and confusion.

A PROBLEM-BUSTING TOOL

Make a To-Do List

When it feels like everyone wants a piece of you and there just aren't enough hours in a day, the simplest way to manage your time is to make a to-do list. List building may seem like a waste of time, literally. That is especially true when you're up against the clock. However, the 10 minutes you spend making the list will bring a sense of calm and you'll most likely feel that everything is achievable. First, write down everything you need to do. Now think about each activity and rank it. Score your tasks from 1 for the least important to 10 for the most important and most urgent tasks. Tackle the number 10 task first. Once that one is out the way, move on to number 9, and so on. Once you get going and can tick off each task, the sense of achievement you get will be far greater than the overwhelming feeling you started with.

The time that you spend making your to-do list will save you time in the long run and keep you on track to complete all your tasks.

STUDIES IN TEEN SURVIVAL

A recent survey found that 49 percent of workers have never conducted a time audit to see how they spend their time. It also found that only one in five people follows a set work schedule. Figuring out how to manage your time can not only help you now, but also improve your productivity in the workplace.

Let's Talk about Stress Management

Stress is a natural response or reaction. It's your body's way of telling you to deal with a challenge or threat. Everyone experiences stress on some level. However, sometimes, life can feel too stressful. School alone brings a lot of pressure. You have coursework, sports, and issues with your friends to deal with. And when you add family life into the mix, life can feel overwhelming.

Defining Self-Management Skills: Stress Management

Everyone feels stressed at times, so it's really important to learn to manage it. Stress management is learning to deal with the pressure and stresses of everyday life. It's learning to deal with the demands that come with day-to-day living. That includes school deadlines and academic work. It also includes doing chores and fitting family time into your schedule. Managing these demands keeps the impact of the stress they might cause as low as possible.

Stress and More Stress

Stress impacts your emotional wellbeing, leaving you feeling anxious or depressed. It can also affect your physical wellbeing. Some people under stress struggle with their sleep, leading them to feel exhausted the next day. And when you're tired, everything feels even more overwhelming than it does after a good night's rest. Added to this, your immune system (the body's system that fights off germs) can be affected by stress too. When you are stressed, you'll be more likely to pick up any bugs that are circulating.

When you're very stressed, your body gets run down and isn't able to fight germs effectively.

Your parents may ask you to do chores around the house. Although this may seem like punishment and a waste of time, the aim is to get you ready to live independently!

Stress Management for the Win

When you learn to deal with stress, you will understand what takes your stress to the next level. You will also know to avoid those triggers or stressors wherever possible. You will understand that when you are stressed, you need to manage your time well and be organized. Being organized will bring a sense of calm, even if you are really busy. And when you're calm, you'll feel happier and healthier, too.

STUDIES IN TEEN SURVIVAL

The American Psychological Association (APA) conducts a stress survey in the United States each year. It consistently shows that teens and young adults show higher levels of stress compared with previous generations. With stress being increasingly prevalent in our modern-day lives, having the skills to manage it is more important than ever.

Journaling can be a great stress-busting tool.

Ways to Beat Stress

So now you know what stress management is, we'll look at the tools you can implement to reduce the impact stress has on your life.

Fit for Anything

One of the easiest things to do when you're stressed is to exercise. You can do something simple like going for a walk. If you feel like more of a challenge, you can go for a run. Joining a gym and signing up for classes is a good way to make sure you do regular exercise. When you exercise more, you'll feel more energetic during the day and you'll sleep better at night.

Eating Healthily

When some people are stressed, they may overeat or crave food that is not healthy. When you're stressed, be aware of not only what you're eating but also why you're eating. Ask yourself if you really are hungry before you eat. Sometimes, we eat just because we are stressed. And when you are hungry, try to choose healthy food like fruit, leafy-green vegetables, and fatty fish such as salmon. All these foods are known to help reduce stress. Make sure you're drinking plenty of water too. If you do drink coffee, try to limit yourself to just one cup in the morning.

Planning Power

Remember in the section on time management, you learned to make a to-do list? Well, when you're stressed, it's more important than ever to write a to-do list and to plan your day. When you plan your day, make sure you schedule time for friends, exercise, and "me-time." Your me-time can include anything that helps you to pause. That might be taking a relaxing bath, listening to music, journaling (see page 21), or meditation.

Find the Stressors

When you feel really stressed, sit and think about what is causing your stress. Are there things that you can change to reduce your stress? If so, those are the things you need to deal with NOW. Don't put them off, just do them right away. Once you've dealt with them, you'll feel a lot better. If there are things you're struggling with and you are not sure how to deal with them, ask for help. Sometimes, just saying your problems out loud can make them seem less of a big deal.

A PROBLEM-BUSTING TOOL

Meditation and Mindfulness

Two great stress-busting tools are meditation and mindfulness. It's a good idea to stop for a moment and refocus your mind, and these two tools allow you to do that. When you're done, you'll feel calmer and happier. If you can, try to build some meditation into your daily routine.
Try these steps:

- Set aside some time to meditate. Early in the morning before you get going and before bedtime are the best times to practice.
- Find somewhere comfortable and something to sit on, such as a rug, yoga mat, or towel. Try to sit up straight.
- Close your eyes, breathe in, and say, "breathe in" in your head. Keep doing this. Once you get used to the idea, you can try a different phrase that works for you.
- Your mind will naturally wander, so when it does, stop, breathe, and say "breathe in" again.

Getting some fresh air and doing some exercise is good for your body and mind.

Let's Talk about Self-Care

When you're younger, you probably had daily routine for eating, sleeping, and keeping clean. As a teenager, you may have less structure, but you still need to take care of yourself. And because you're a teenager, there's definitely more to this than brushing your teeth!

Defining Self-Management Skills: Self-Care

Self-care means looking after yourself. That may sound basic, but there are different parts to self-care that you need to learn and understand to feel physically and mentally healthy. These include physical, mental and emotional, creative, and spiritual self-care.

The Physical Stuff

By now you'll know the benefits of exercising. A little bit of exercise each day is great for your body. It doesn't have to be a run on your own. Think about going for a walk with your friend, or visiting a skatepark for a while. You can also take part in school or club sports and play some soccer or swim. With all this physical activity, remember to practice good personal hygiene. Keep your body clean by showering after sport and washing your hair regularly. When you have time, shower for longer or have a bath. That will help you to relax as well as keep clean.

STUDIES IN TEEN SURVIVAL

In 2023, psychologists completed a survey of teenagers in the United States. The survey found that more than 90 percent of those surveyed used self-care tools to manage their mental health and emotions. More than 70 percent of the teenagers said that they listened to music as their main way to care for their mental and emotional health.

The Mental Stuff

Caring for your mind means doing the things you enjoy. That might be watching a movie or your favorite TV show. It might be listening to music. Some people enjoy being outside in nature: going for a walk or hike. Friends are especially important to teenagers and their mental wellbeing. It's great to have a friend to talk to and laugh with.

The Creative Stuff

Flexing your creative muscles is just as good as working on your actual muscles! You might like listening to music, drawing, or taking photos. Some people like to learn too. This doesn't mean sitting with your nose in a book studying. It means following a recipe to learn how to cook a new dish, listening to interesting podcasts, or reading a book that takes you to another world.

Not everyone is creative but sometimes, stepping out of your comfort zone and trying a creative activity will leave you feeling like you've achieved a lot.

WHY SELF-MANAGEMENT WORKS

You've discovered skills that will see you through school, college, and into your career. They include setting goals, self-motivation, time management, and stress management. Let's take one more look at the value they bring.

1

Setting Goals Keeps You Focused

Teenagers who set goals are more focused. They work hard to meet their short-term and long-term goals without the fear of failure stopping them.

2

Self-Motivation Builds Self-Esteem

Knowing that you are working hard toward something, and persevering to achieve it, brings a great sense of self-belief and self-esteem.

3

Time Management Brings Calm

Time management involves working through things to get tasks done on time and efficiently. When you are organized and have structure in your day, it will feel less chaotic and calmer.

4 Stress Management Protects Your Body and Mind

Stress can make you physically and mentally sick so it's important to keep on top of it. Simple tools, from sleeping and eating well to understanding the things that make you feel stressed, can help.

5 Self-Care Keeps You Healthy Too

When you look after yourself physically, emotionally, and spiritually, you will feel less stressed and more in control of your daily life.

Kindness Is Key

At school and later at work, you'll encounter different types of people. Some you'll instantly like and get on with, but others you won't. That's life. However, it's important to be a kind human. Try to be thoughtful, respectful, and considerate of other people's thoughts and feelings. It's also a good thing to be kind to yourself. Try to be accepting of your weaknesses, and learn from them.

CHAPTER 4

Friendships and the Wider World

People are designed to work together as a group. We all need each other and we are all part of something bigger and larger than just ourselves. This is where your friends and people in the wider world come into the discussion.

Friends Forever

As a teenager, your friendships are becoming more important than ever. Gone are the days when you're happy to just be at home with your family. Your friends share your interests, thoughts, and values. You're learning about yourself and each other by being together, and you're also finding your place in the world through your friendships.

It's a Big, Small World

Before social media exploded and everyone was on a chat group or posting reels, the world was big place. It took time and a lot of effort to keep in contact with friends who were far away. Today, the world is a lot smaller thanks to all the technology available. But though tech helps us keep in touch, it can increase our stress levels, affect our sleep, and affect our relationships too. That's why it's important to carefully manage the time that we spend on social media.

Tech brings people closer than ever before but it can also bring problems.

Watching your favorite show can be relaxing but binge-watching an entire series may not be the best use of your time.

Keeping Safe

Now that you are a teenager your focus has likely changed from your immediate area to a big, wide world available to you through social media. While that is exciting, it also brings dangers. That is why staying safe on social media is important. Following these rules will help you stay safe while you are online:

- Always be aware of those you are in contact with.
- Talk only to people you know. That means you know where they live, you've met them in person, and your parents know who they are.
- Don't give away personal details to strangers.
- Keep your address, school, and family information private.
- Don't send photos, reels, or longer videos you may regret later—even if it's to friends that you trust.
- If there is something that makes you feel uncomfortable, whether it affects you or someone else, talk to a trusted adult.

Being in Control

Remember to include screen time when you plan your day. Otherwise, you can find yourself spending too much time looking at a screen. Another way to be in control of tech is to be present. Don't be distracted when you're supposed to be studying or sleeping. Set rules so it's less distracting—for example, no devices during dinner and no social media during homework time. And lastly, choose real life over tech. Meet up with your friends, walk with them, and talk to them in person when possible rather than through a device. Face-to-face, in-person chats with a friend are always better than conversations held online.

Let's Talk about Decision Making

There are many parts of being a young child that were great. Your parents did a lot for you. They decided what you ate, who you had playdates with, and what TV you watched. Each day, they made many decisions for you. But now, as a teenager, you need to make decisions for yourself, and that can be difficult. Learning how to make good decisions can make the process a lot easier. And we'll next explore how to do that.

Sometimes, deciding to do something can feel like jumping off a cliff into the unknown. But you can learn from these challenges.

Defining Self-Management Skills: Decision Making

If decision making was just saying yes or no to something, life would be so easy. Unfortunately, it's not! Decision making is about weighing up all the options and choosing the one that is more suitable. To make a good decision, you need to see the bigger picture so that you understand potential issues and what the impact of your solution will be. For example, sometimes you need to decide whether or not to take a risk. It may result in a good outcome or it may bring about a bad one. Carefully weighing up the potential outcomes before you take risks will help you make good decisions.

STUDIES IN TEEN SURVIVAL

Research shows that young people who are supported to participate in decision making are more likely to have increased confidence and self-belief, exercise positive career choices, and have greater involvement and responsibility in the future.

The Self-Management Workshop

Making Poor Decisions

Let's take a look at what happens when decision making is not good. Imagine you have moved to a new town, and don't have many friends. So at school, you sit next to two guys at lunchtime, and they start to talk to you. You get on well, and a few days later they ask you to meet them at the mall. "It'll be fun!" they say. But you feel uncomfortable when you see them laughing as you head off to your next class. You don't have a good gut feeling. But you ignore it, and meet them at the mall after school. You go into a skate store and start browsing. One of the guys moves close to you and says, "You watch the security officer while I stuff my bag." You really want to belong, so you say, "Got it." You don't realize that there are two security officers, and you are all caught.

Let's look at the issues here: You didn't get good gut feeling but you ignored it. With some more thought about the situation before agreeing to go along with it, you'd likely make better decisions. Don't underestimate the value of trusting your gut...

THE SELF-MANAGEMENT WORKSHOP

Same situation, but with good decisions.

Going with Your Gut

Your two new friends ask you to meet them at the mall, but you feel uncomfortable when you see them laughing as you head off to your next class. You don't have a good gut feeling. You think carefully about it and decide to go along, but ask your mom to keep her phone close in case you need her to fetch you early. You meet the guys, go into a skate store, and start browsing. One of the guys moves close to you and says, "You watch the security officer while I stuff my bag." You really want to belong, but you know stealing is wrong. So you reply, "No, I'm good thanks. I'll catch you at school." You walk out of the store and phone your mom to fetch you.

What Works Better Here?:

- You listen to your gut, and trust the feeling.
- You don't feel comfortable, so you make a plan B.
- You don't want to take a bad risk, so you walk away.

Good Decision Making—What Can It Do for You?

When you have a decision to make, take your time and think things through. Understand the consequences of your decision. Is the risk worth taking? If so, act on your decision and evaluate the outcome afterward.

When your gut tells you that something is not right, listen to it, and walk away from the situation.

A PROBLEM-BUSTING TOOL

Pros and Cons Lists

When you have a big decision to make, create a list. Set up a table with "pros" on one side and "cons" on the other. Think things through, filling out the columns. When you're done, look to see which side has the most points. Make your decision and then sleep on it. In the morning, think about your decision. Do you still feel the same way?

Peer Pressure Is Real

Your peers are the teenagers who are a similar age to you. You'll probably share some common interests with them. Perhaps you're on the same teams or in the same clubs. It's natural for teenagers to want to fit in with others, especially when they're the teens everyone wants to be like.

Good Friends Are Great

Being part of a friendship circle gives teenagers a feeling of belonging and acceptance. Friends with qualities that you admire, such as kindness, will also have a good influence on you—you'll be kind too. Good friends also give you feedback. They may help you when you struggle with something and will be there for you when there are problems. They'll talk through tough decisions so that you make the right choices.

Not So Positive

Not all friendships are great. Sometimes, your friends may pressure you to do something that you're uncomfortable doing. They may expect you to drink alcohol, vape, or steal. Because people want to feel like they belong, they may go along with these friends and do as they do, just to be accepted.

Hanging out with friends who have similar interests to you is a great way to relax and have some fun.

People may feel they've found their tribe by joining a gang, but gang life is dangerous. They will be forced to do things that they would never normally do.

Getting It Right

So how do you know when to go along with your friends and when to steer clear? The first thing is to listen to your gut. If it feels uncomfortable or wrong, it probably is not right for you. Plan ahead and be prepared. For example, if you go to a party and you think someone will offer you a vape, plan in your head what you'll say and how you'll act. Know what you're comfortable with and go with that. Remember, it's OK to say no. Good friends will understand and not pressure you into doing something you're uncomfortable with.

Teen Need to Know

Teenagers are often under pressure to fit in. Gangs often offer vulnerable teens a chance to fit in and feel part of a "family," with a sense of belonging. Gang leaders use peer pressure to intimidate people to join, forcing them or daring them to join their gang. Sometimes, the peer pressure is not so aggressive. The gang members often attract others by appearing to have a great lifestyle—one that teens think looks great. When a gang member is friendly or kind to someone, they may feel a sense of belonging and then join the gang.

Let's Talk about Community Belonging

A community is a group of people who live in the same place or a group of people who have similar interests or characteristics in common. Being a part of a community is really important because it creates a sense of belonging. When you're active in your community, you'll feel a sense of togetherness and a great pride in your group.

Taking part in a community project brings a feeling of belonging. It also creates a sense of pride in the community.

Defining Self-Management Skills: Community Belonging

For a community to flourish and work well, everyone has to play their part and be responsible. When you belong to a community, you have to work with others to achieve a positive outcome. Members of a healthy community feel valued, included, and connected to each other.

New Skills, New Friends

Being part of a community will teach you valuable lessons. You'll learn to be responsible for yourself and others. The community will flourish because people care about others and they respect them. Everyone brings something different to a community so you'll learn new skills too. You'll also make new friends and having a group of friends will build your confidence and self-esteem.

Part of the Civic System

Being a part of a community is not all about having fun. When you're part of a community, there are certain things you have to do. Each and every member of the community has to play their part and do their duty. These obligations are known as civic duties. For adults, the duties include obeying the law, serving on juries, voting, paying taxes, and upholding the constitution. As a teenager, you may not have the same civic duties to perform. However, you can start to learn about how civic systems and structures work. That way, when you have to do your civic duty, you will know what to expect.

Get Involved!

Belonging to a community, means being involved and playing your part. You can do this with some simple, but effective, steps. Try to find an organization in your community that you feel inspired by and volunteer to help there when you can. Animal shelters, feeding schemes, and children's homes are always looking for volunteers. If you can't spare the time, see if you can do something else to help them. Collect bags of dog food for the shelter, canned food for the feeding scheme, and old toys for the children's home. There are plenty of ways to help when you think about it.

Helping your neighbor—perhaps by walking their dog—is a great way to be a part of a community.

WHY SELF-MANAGEMENT WORKS

You made it to the end of the book and you've got some great skills to help you manage your life. Let's revisit decision making and community belonging to see what they can do for you.

1 Thinking Through Decisions Is a Step Toward Independence

Being able to think through your decisions to make what you feel is the right decision is an important step in becoming more independent.

2 Positive Peer Pressure Can Help You Grow

When you hang out with people who are similar to you and have the same beliefs and goals, it can have a positive impact on your life.

3 Negative Peer Pressure Can Damage You

When you try to fit into a group of teenagers who are different from you, you may face peer pressure to do things that you aren't comfortable doing. That is never a good thing.

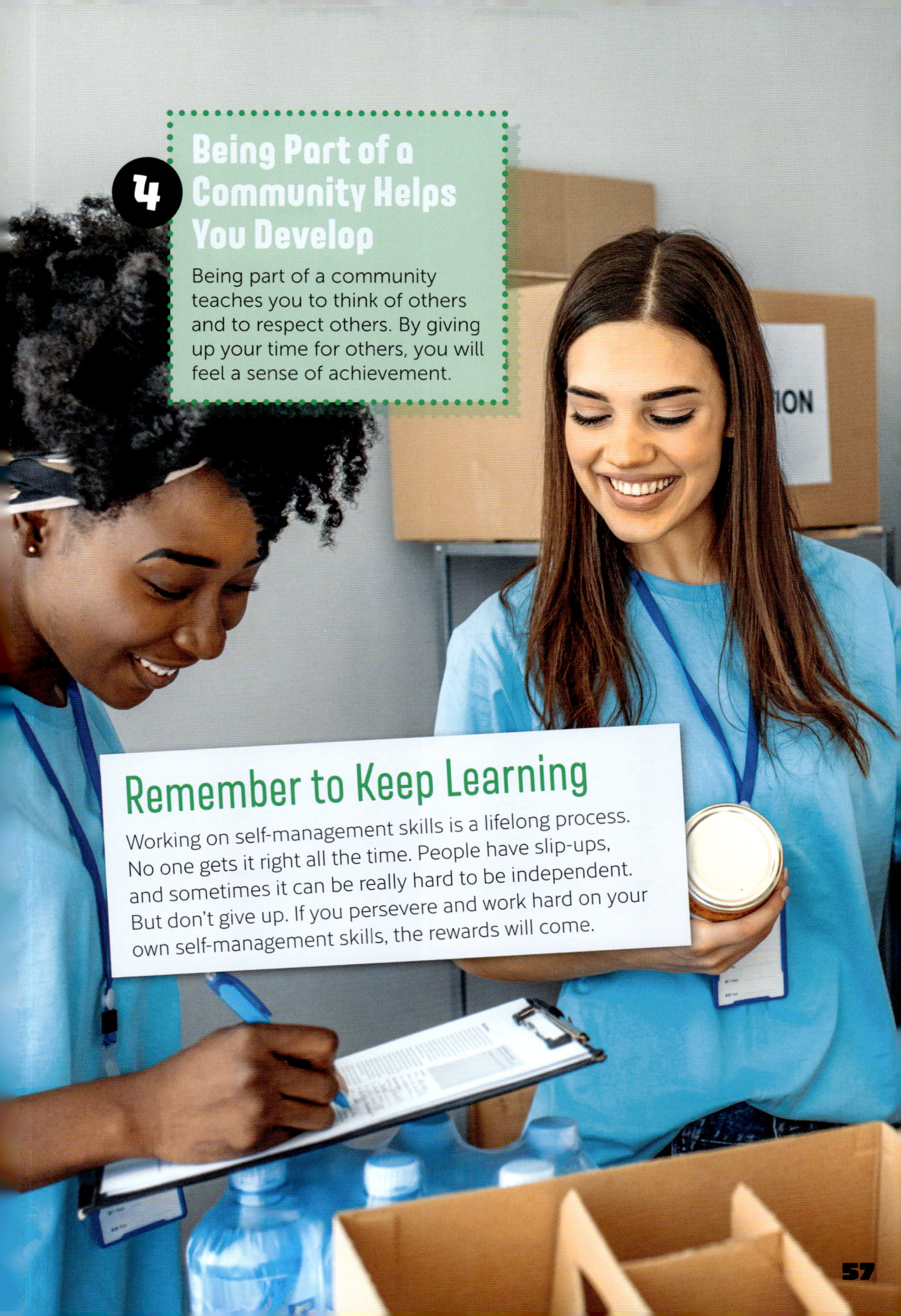

4 Being Part of a Community Helps You Develop

Being part of a community teaches you to think of others and to respect others. By giving up your time for others, you will feel a sense of achievement.

Remember to Keep Learning

Working on self-management skills is a lifelong process. No one gets it right all the time. People have slip-ups, and sometimes it can be really hard to be independent. But don't give up. If you persevere and work hard on your own self-management skills, the rewards will come.

CONCLUSION

Skills for Life

Now that you are equipped with self-management skills, keep using them and practicing them as much as you can. Keep a journal and take note of what works well and what helps you feel more independent. What can you do to be less reliant on others? Consider what you think you could improve, and how you feel as a result. And to set you on your way, here are some important guidelines to help steer your course.

Don't Forget to Reflect

Self-reflection will help you keep track of what you are thinking and feeling, and how that may be affecting your relationships. When you take time out to think calmly about what is going on with your thoughts and emotions, you can then act on that information.

Keep Talking

Honest, open communication is the key. Keep talking to the people you care about and share how you feel. Remember, if they don't know how you are feeling and what you are thinking, they won't be able to help you with any issues.

If in Doubt, Ask

If you are unsure how to manage a situation, ask a trusted adult to help. Parents, teachers, and counselors are all there to help when the going gets tough. They have had years of practice working on their own self-management skills, so draw on their knowledge and experience.

Taking the time to sit and think things through may seem a little odd at first, but it's a great way to stay on top of things and to stay focused. And don't be afraid to ask for help from others if you need it.

Mastering self-management tools now before you enter the workplace will set you up for the rest of your life.

Keep Going

Learning self-management skills can give you a real sense of achievement, especially when you become more independent. But remember, there may be bumps along the way and the best way to deal with the bumps is to talk them through with a friend or trusted adult. Share your ideas and what you think.

Share Your Skills

Remember to share what you've learned with friends and family. You've learned some powerful tools, and are in a position to help others work on their self-management skills. Spread your newfound knowledge and insights!

Glossary

adolescence the time of life when someone goes through the process of changing from a child into an adult

aggressive describes an overly forceful approach

anxious nervous or worried

benefits the advantages a person gains from something

binge-watching watching an entire series in one sitting

blended families families that include stepsiblings and parents, and halfsiblings

chaotic describes something that is disordered and confused

comfort zone a situation or position where a person feels secure, comfortable, and in control

communication sharing information with others

compromise a situation in which people consider and accept some of the wishes of other people

confidence a person's sense of security in their abilities, qualities, or ideas

conflict a disagreement or argument

cons negative outcomes

consequences the results and effects of something

consideration careful thought about something

demands requests to do things

depressed describes someone who has a low mood and lack of interest in most activities

determination having a strong desire to do or achieve something

effectively working well

embrace to accept or believe in something

engagement an arrangement to do something

facial expressions the ways a person's face changes depending on the emotions they feel

feedback comments about how well or badly something has been done and how it can be improved

flourish to be successful

fulfilled feeling complete and that something has been achieved

generations people who are a similar age and who have similar experiences and attitudes

gut feeling a feeling based on instinct or emotion

hormones chemicals in the body that help the organs function properly

implement to put something into practice

impulsive carrying out action without thinking carefully about it beforehand

independently without help

informed describes a decision that has been thought through

meditation a practice of calming the mind and body

mindfulness a practice in which a person trains their mind to focus on the present

overwhelmed feeling overpowered by emotions and thoughts

ownership taking responsibility for something

persevere to carry on

potential a positive state that can be achieved

pride a feeling of satisfaction in something

prioritize to put something first

pros positive outcomes

psychologists professionals who study the human mind and the behaviors and thoughts of people

rank to put something in order

reflect to think carefully about something that has happened

routine a series of things that a person does in a particular order

schedule a plan of events or tasks that states when each one is done

self-confidence a person's belief in their abilities

siblings brothers and sisters

stepmother the woman someone's father marries if their parents are divorced or their mother has passed away

stepsibling the child of a stepparent

stressors things that trigger stress

triggers the things that cause a certain reaction

uncertainty doubt about things

values morals and beliefs

visualize to picture something

volunteer to offer to do something without being forced to do it

Find Out More

BOOKS

Knight, B.A. *Life Skills for Teens Made Simple: 10 Rock-solid ways to unleash unshakable confidence, efficiently manage time and money, sharpen your cooking prowess, and much more for a stress-free life.* Arm in Arm Publishing, 2024.

Meyer, Jaqui. *Adulting Life Skills for Young Adults: Beyond the Basics: Tools to Navigate Through High School, College, and Into the World with Inner Knowledge and the Ability to Thrive.* IRIS Innovatives, 2023.

WEBSITES

Find out more about mindfulness and how to be less stressed at:
www.changetochill.org

Take control of your mental health with a little help from Mental Health Is Health:
www.mentalhealthishealth.us

ORGANIZATIONS

For more help with self-management, take a look at this organization:

The Jed Foundation, 745 Fifth Avenue Suite 500, New York, NY 10151
+ 212 647 7544
Website: https://jedfoundation.org

Publisher's note to educators and parents:
All the websites featured above have been carefully reviewed to ensure that they are suitable for students. However, many websites change often, and we cannot guarantee that a site's future contents will continue to meet our high standards of educational value. Please be advised that students should be closely monitored whenever they access the Internet.

Index

About the Author

Jennifer Sanderson has written books on many different topics, from tennis and baby animals to geography and self-care. She has two teenagers who, like all young people, are learning to navigate life's ups and downs by becoming more independent. She's hoping this book will give them and other readers the skills they need to go from the roller coaster of being teenagers to fully-fledged self-managing adults.